EXTRA THICK EASY LINE COLORING BOOK

CRYSTAL
COLORING BOOKS

ISBN: 9781086973259

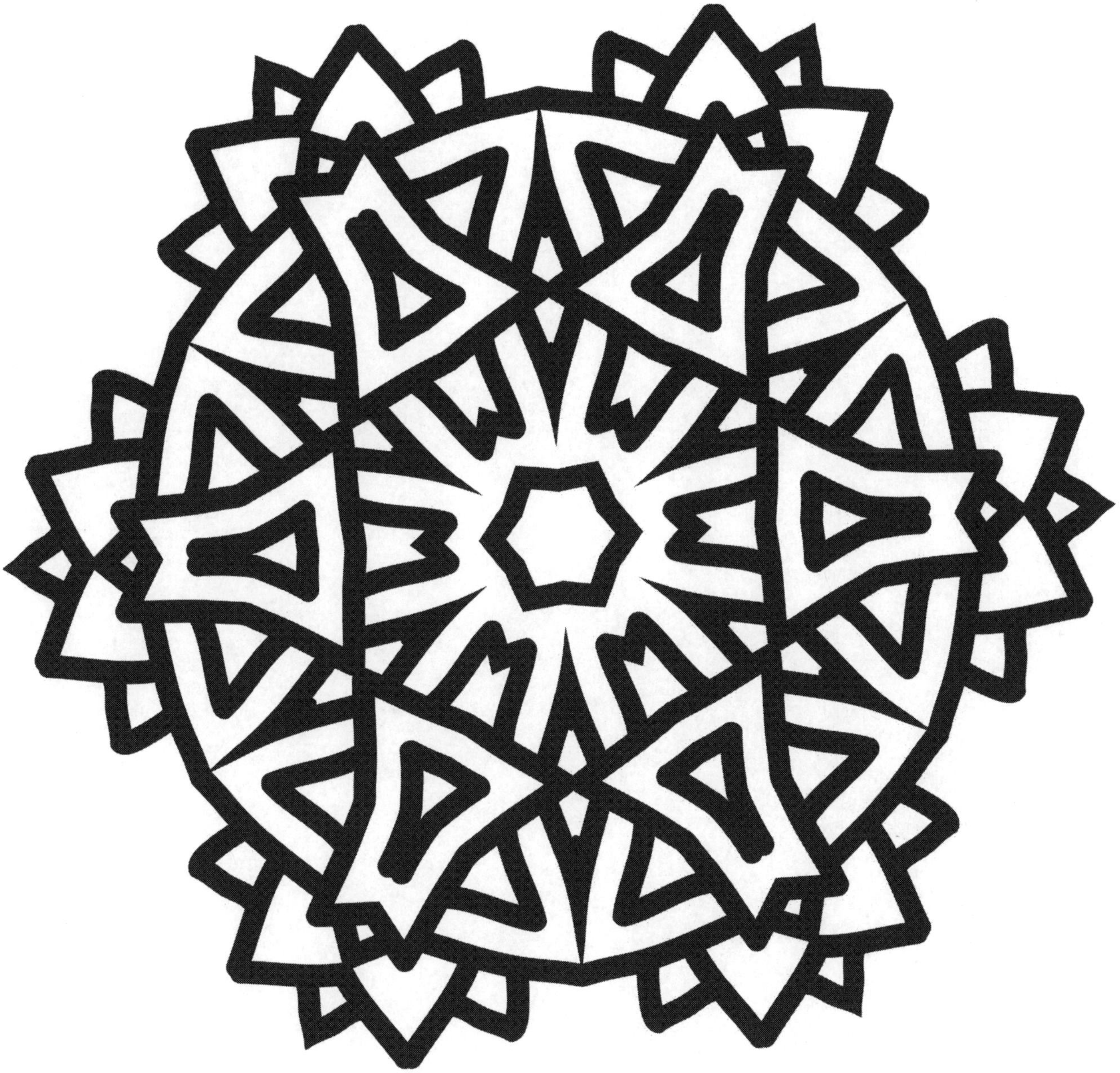

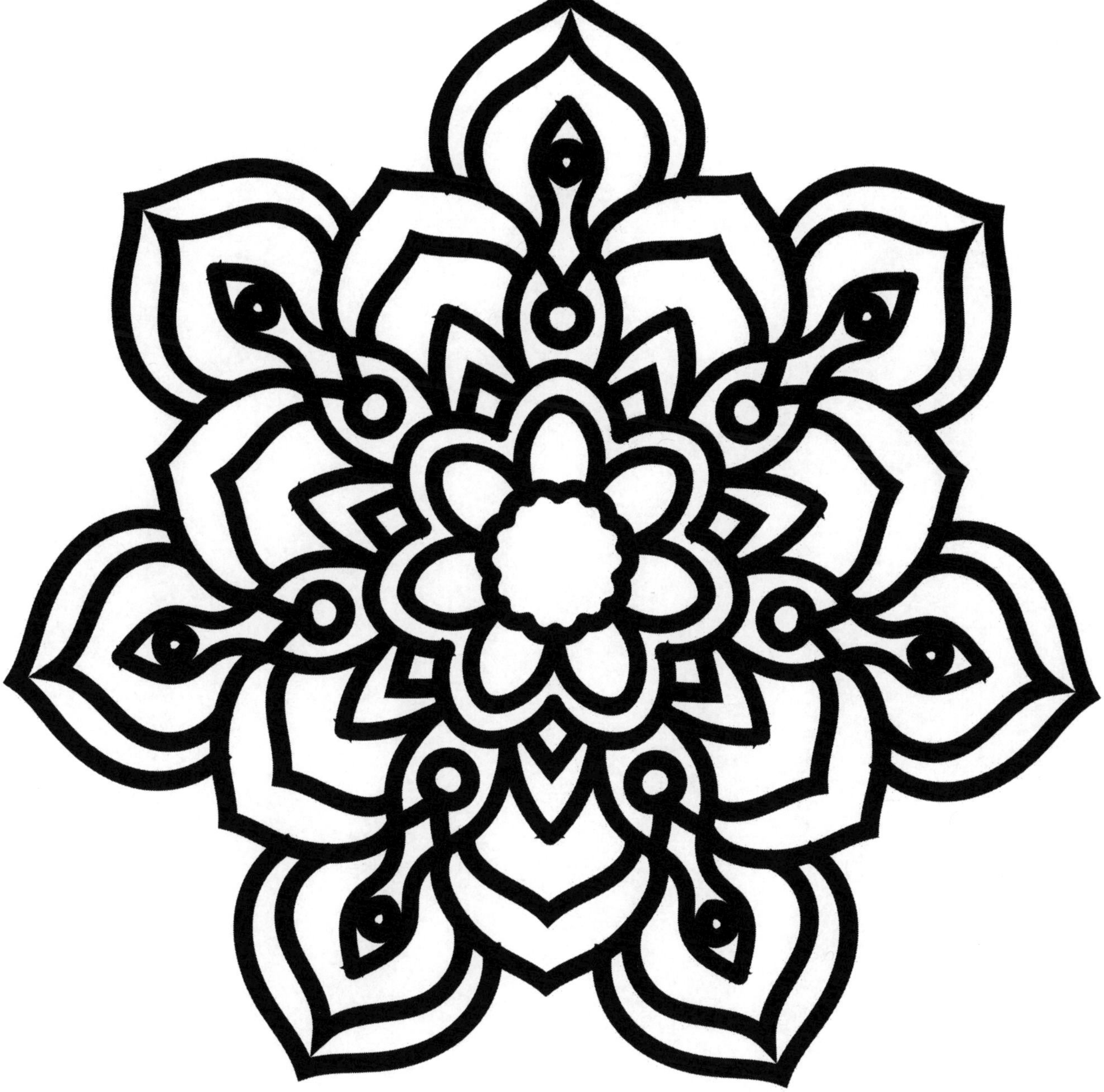

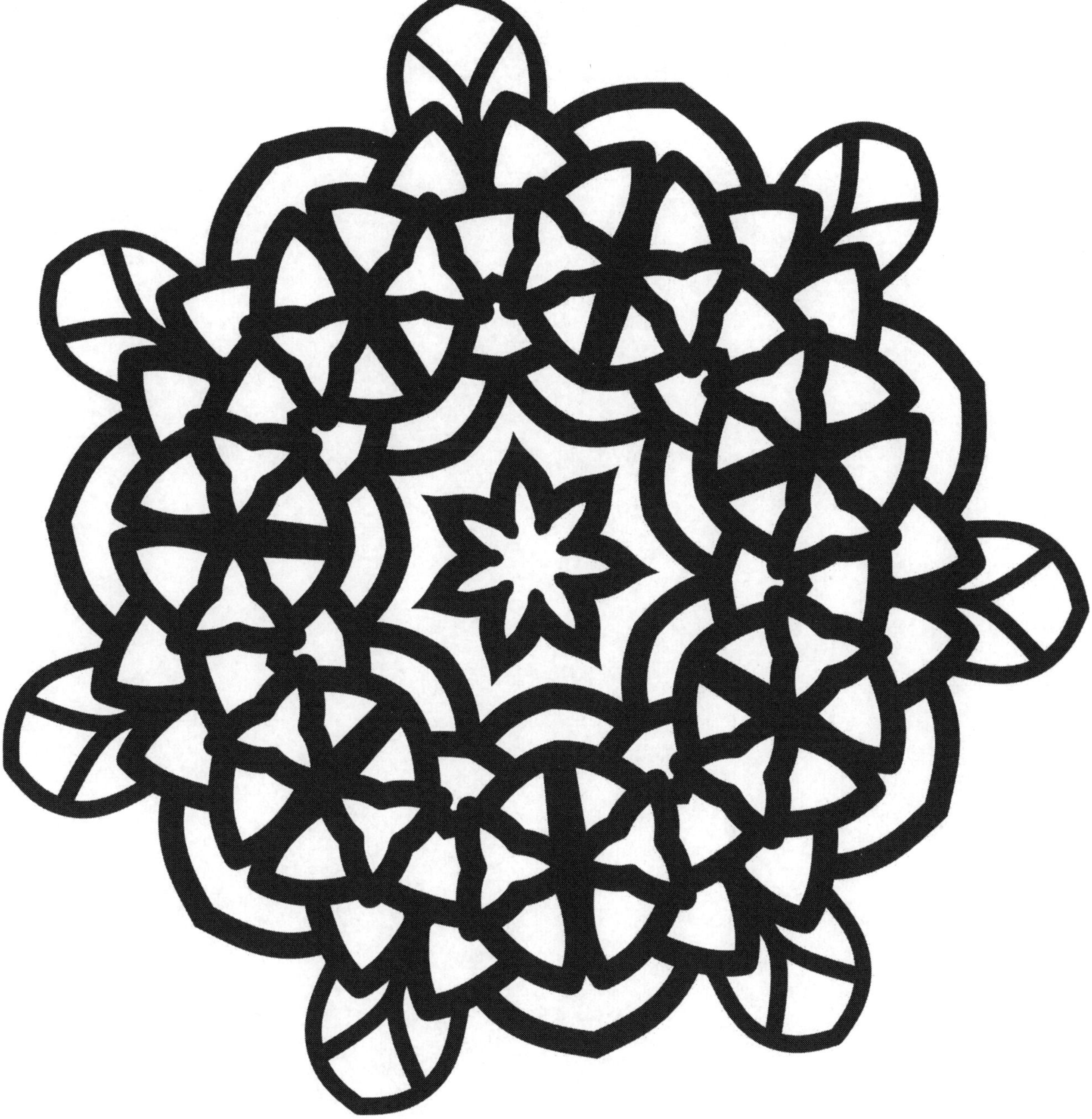

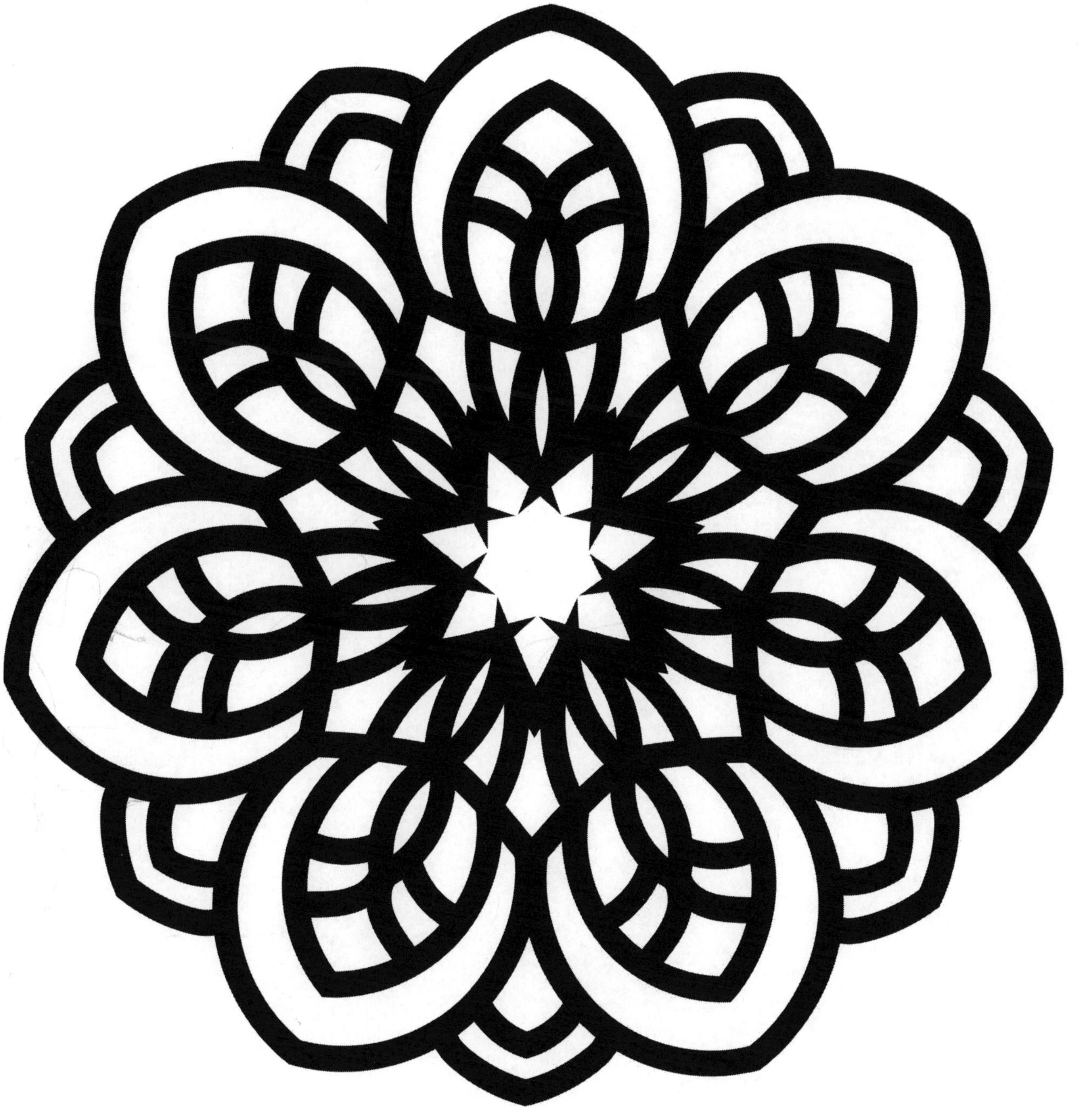

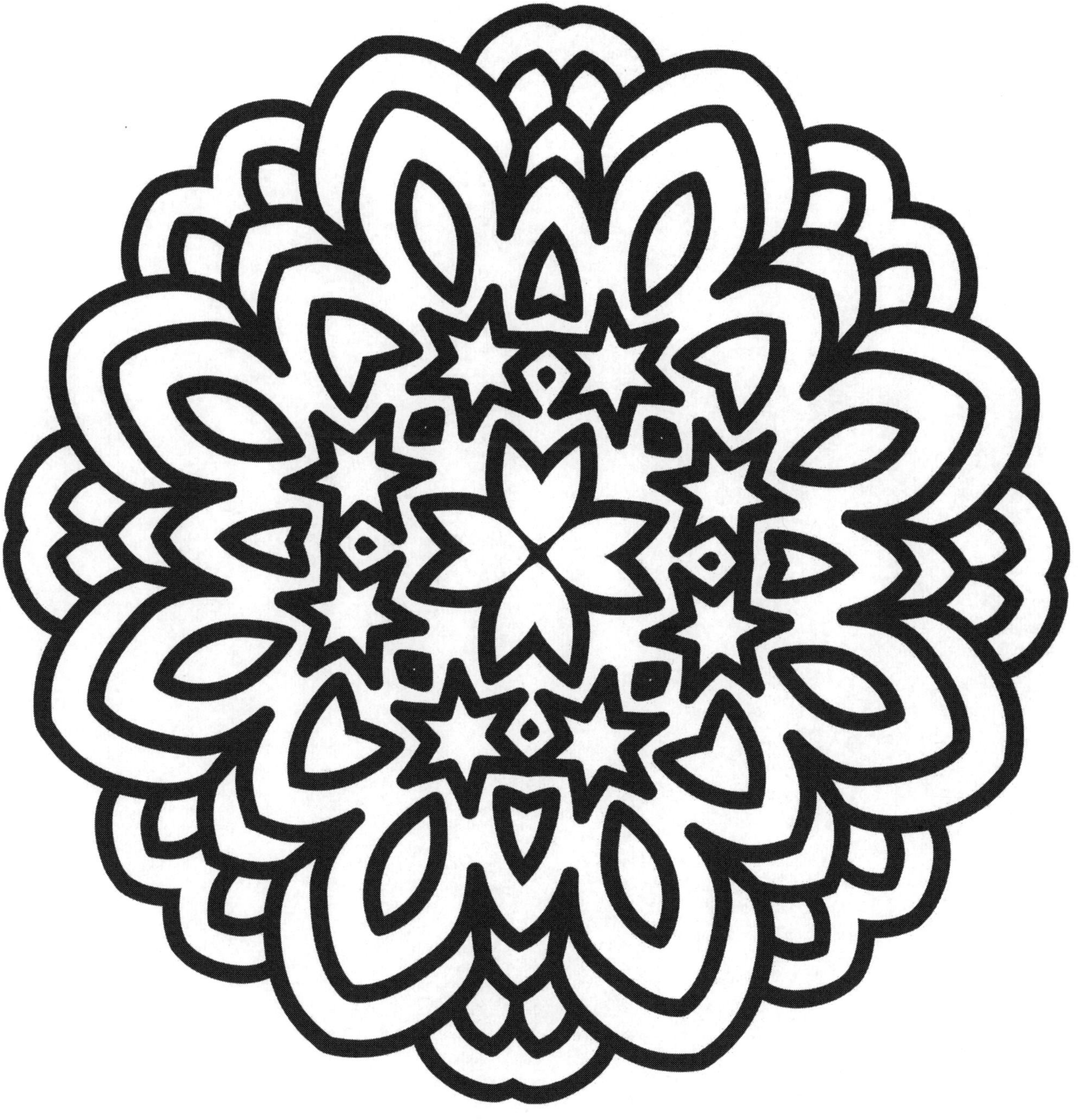

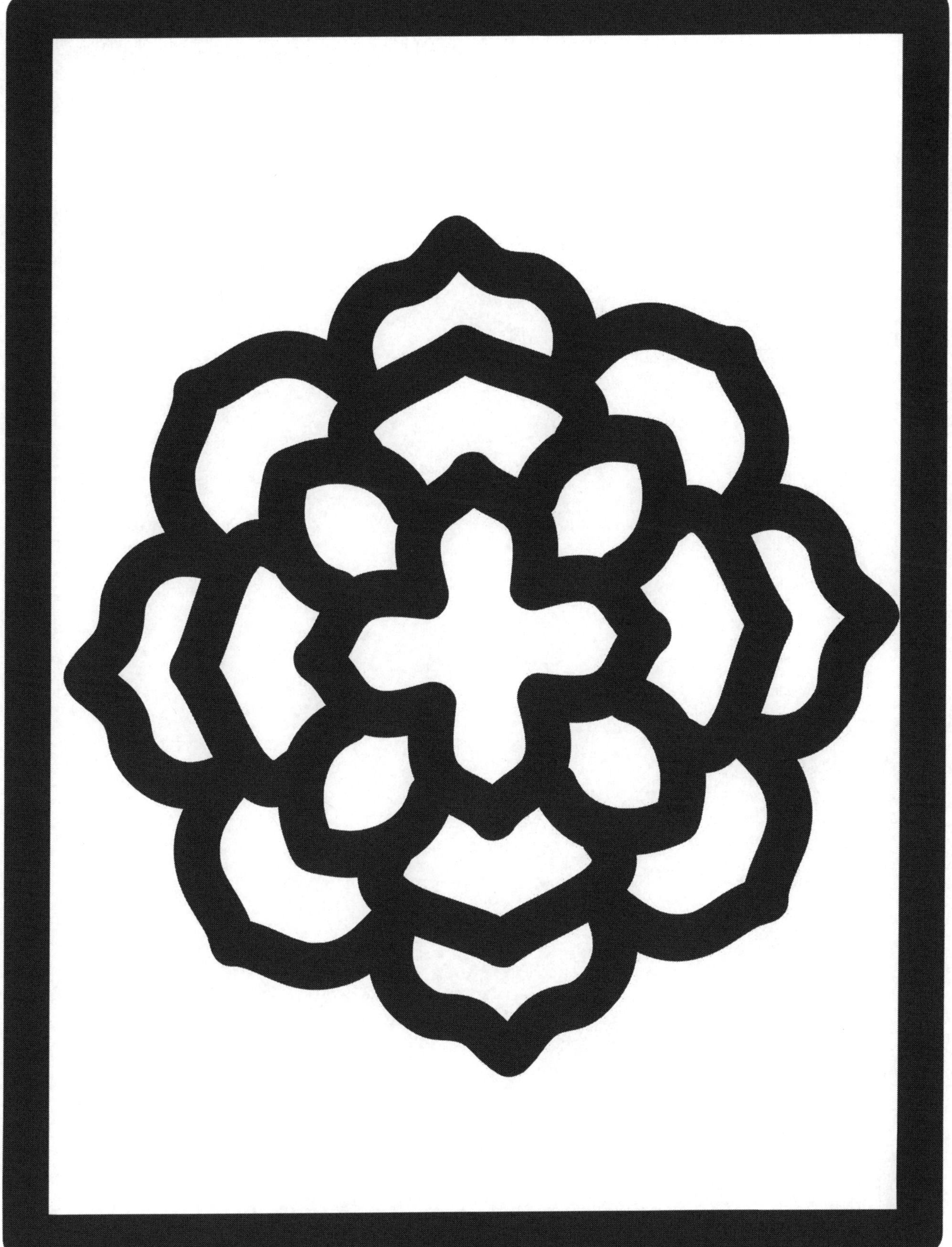

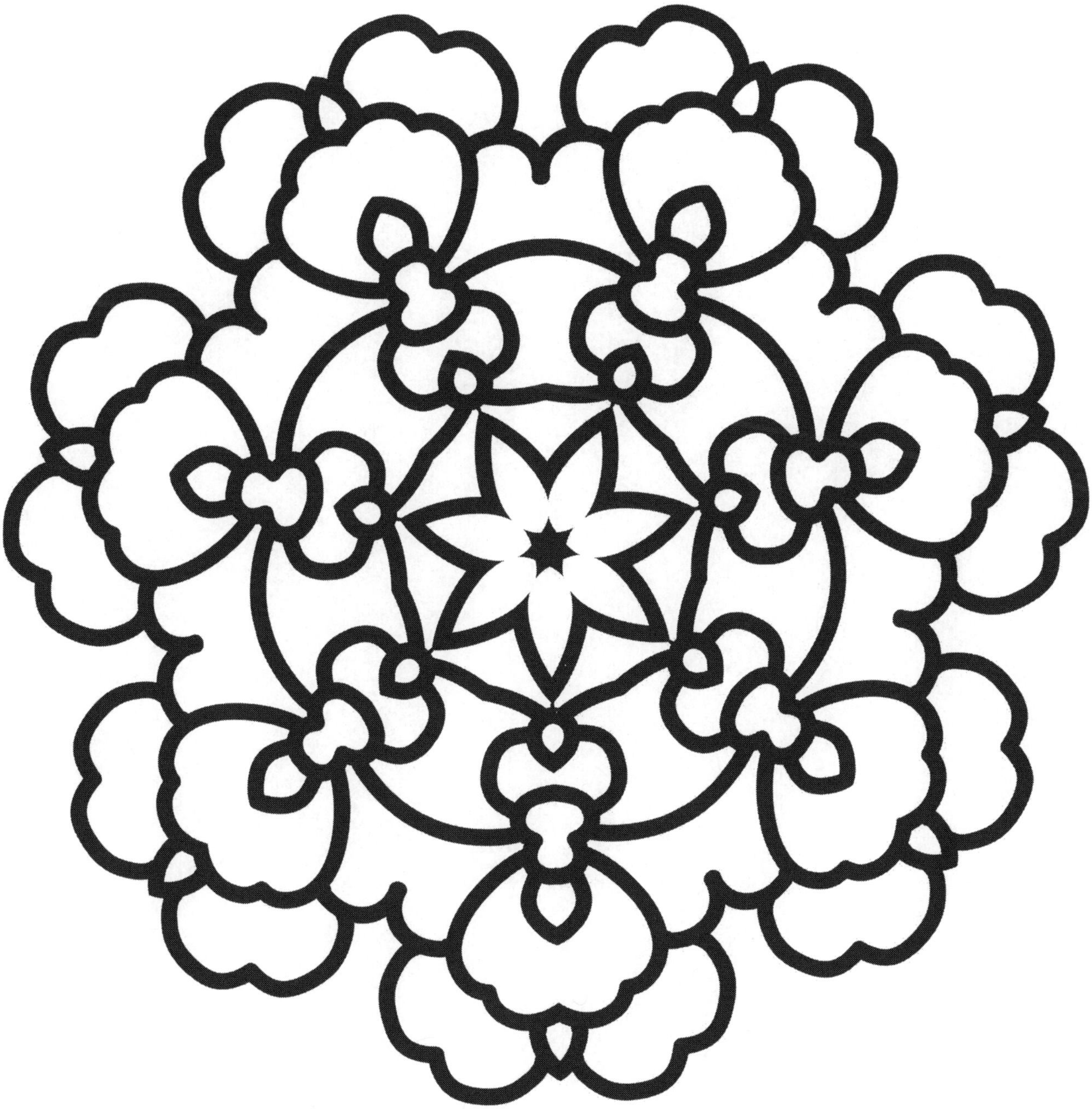

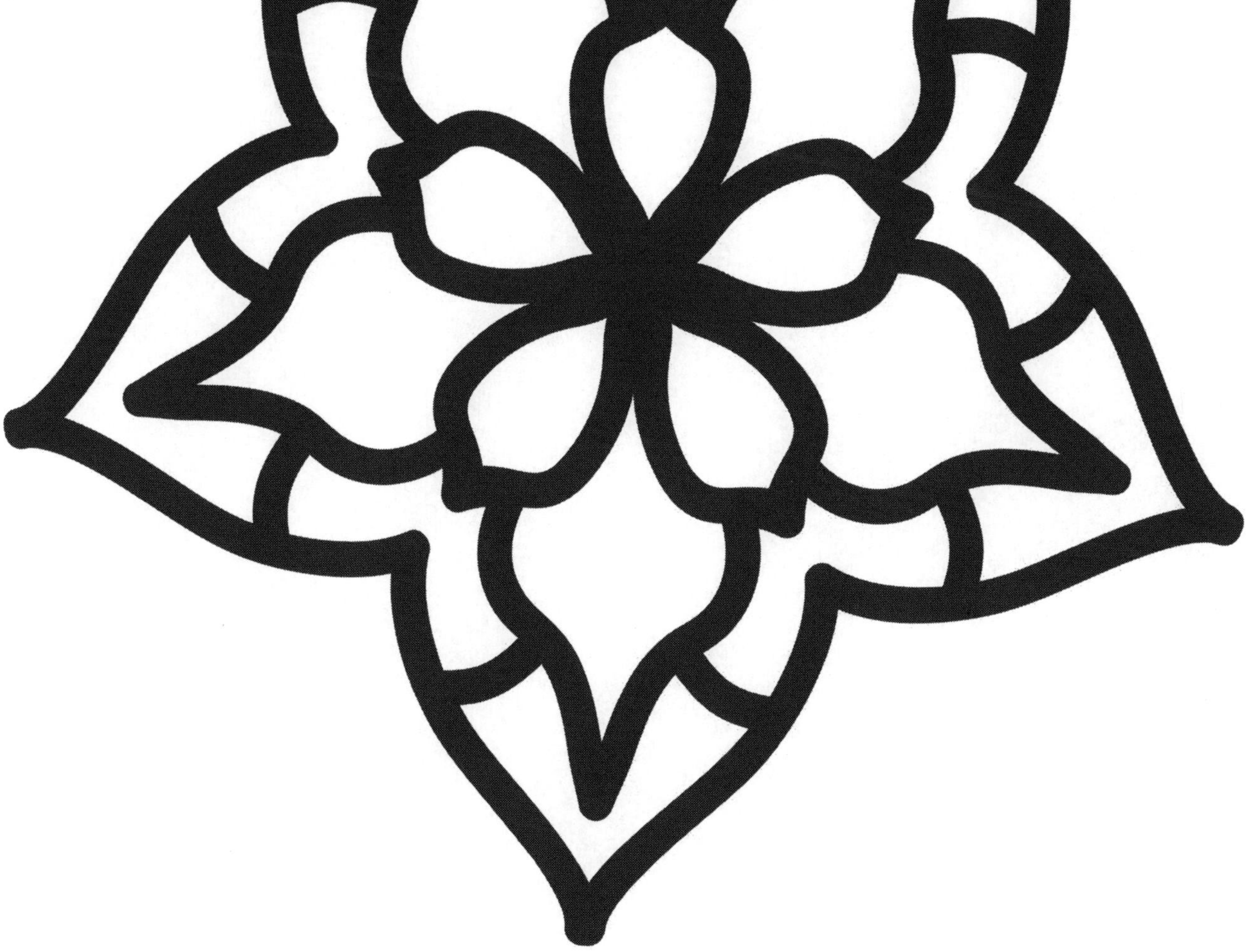

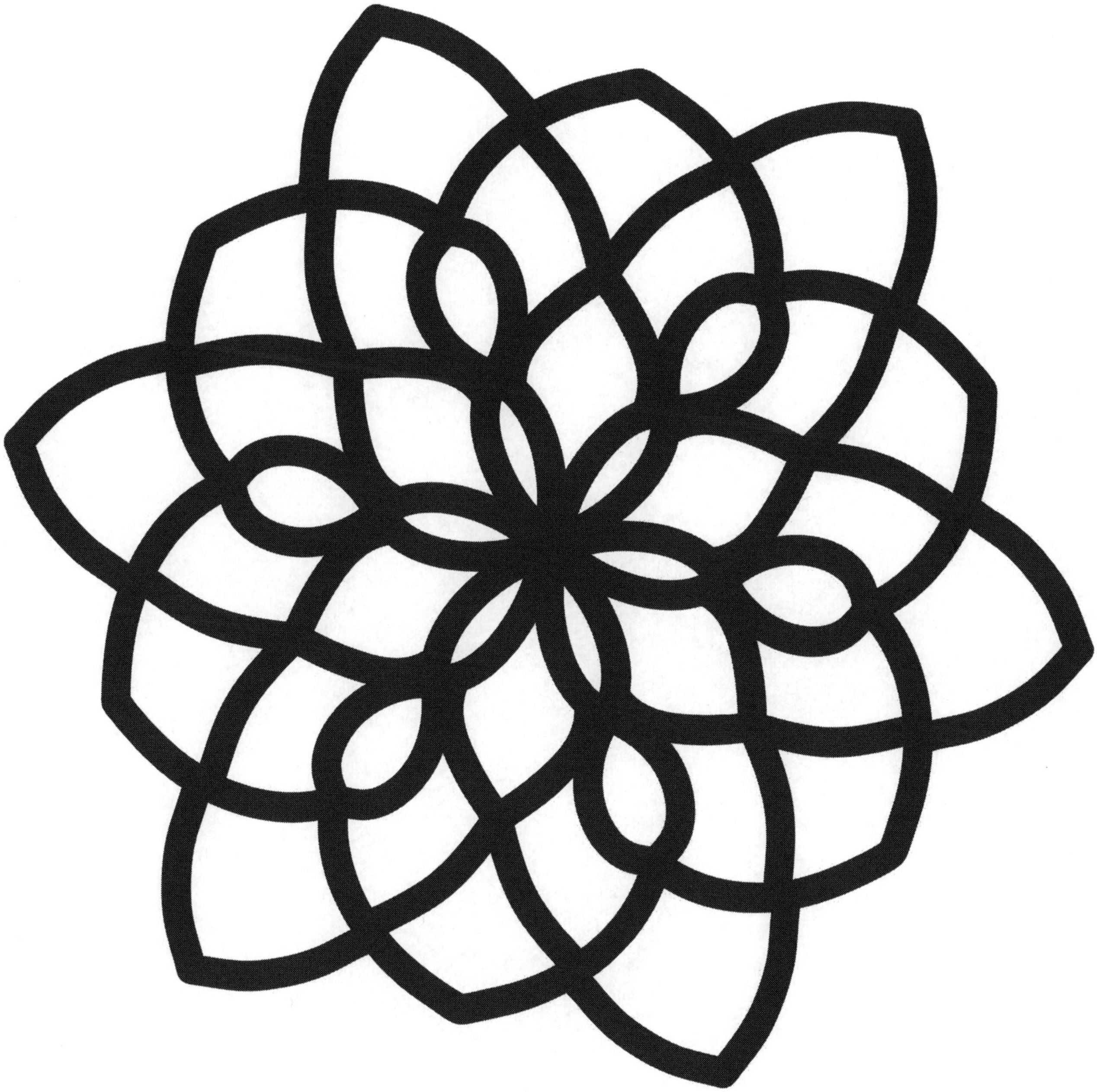

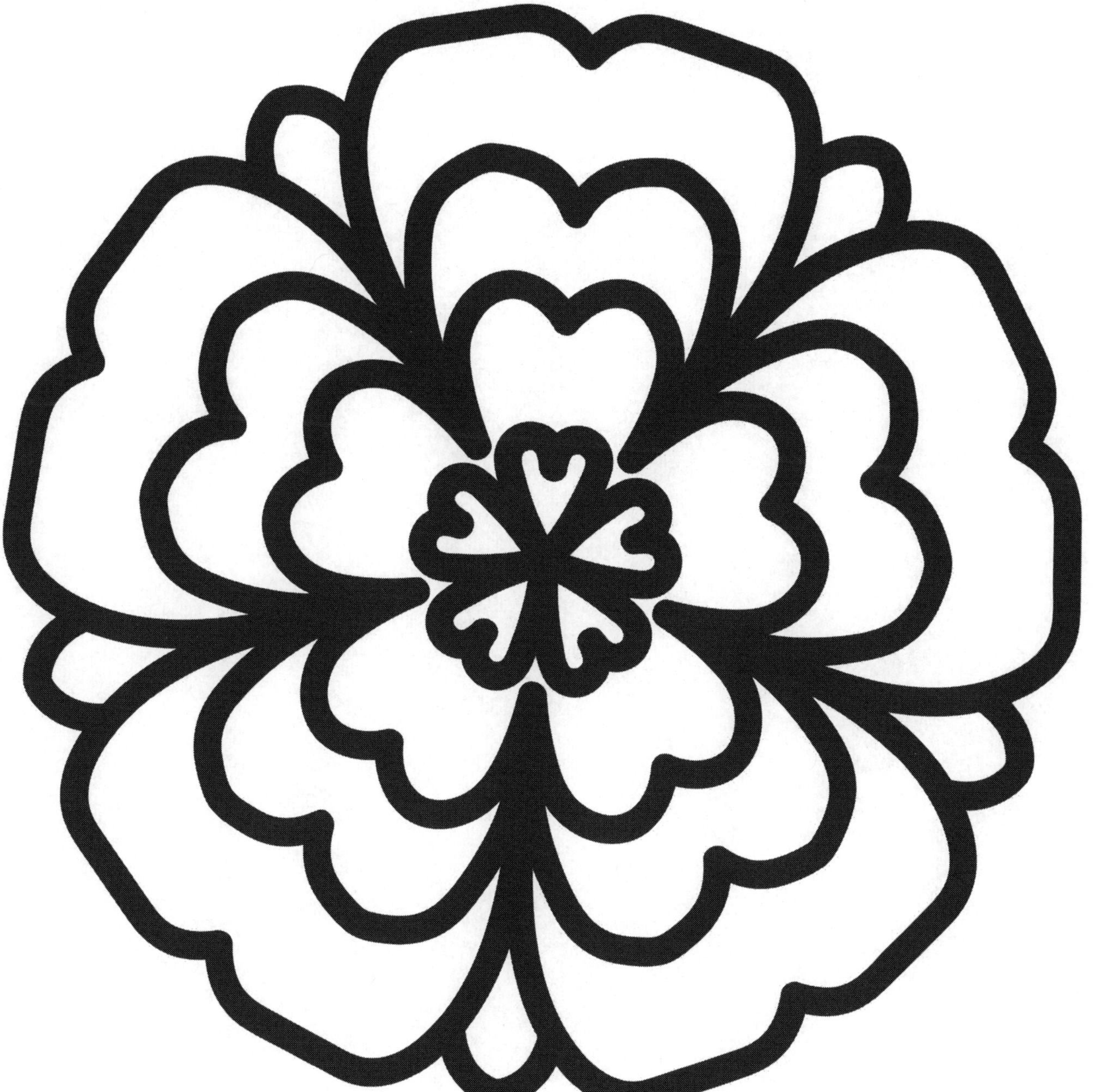

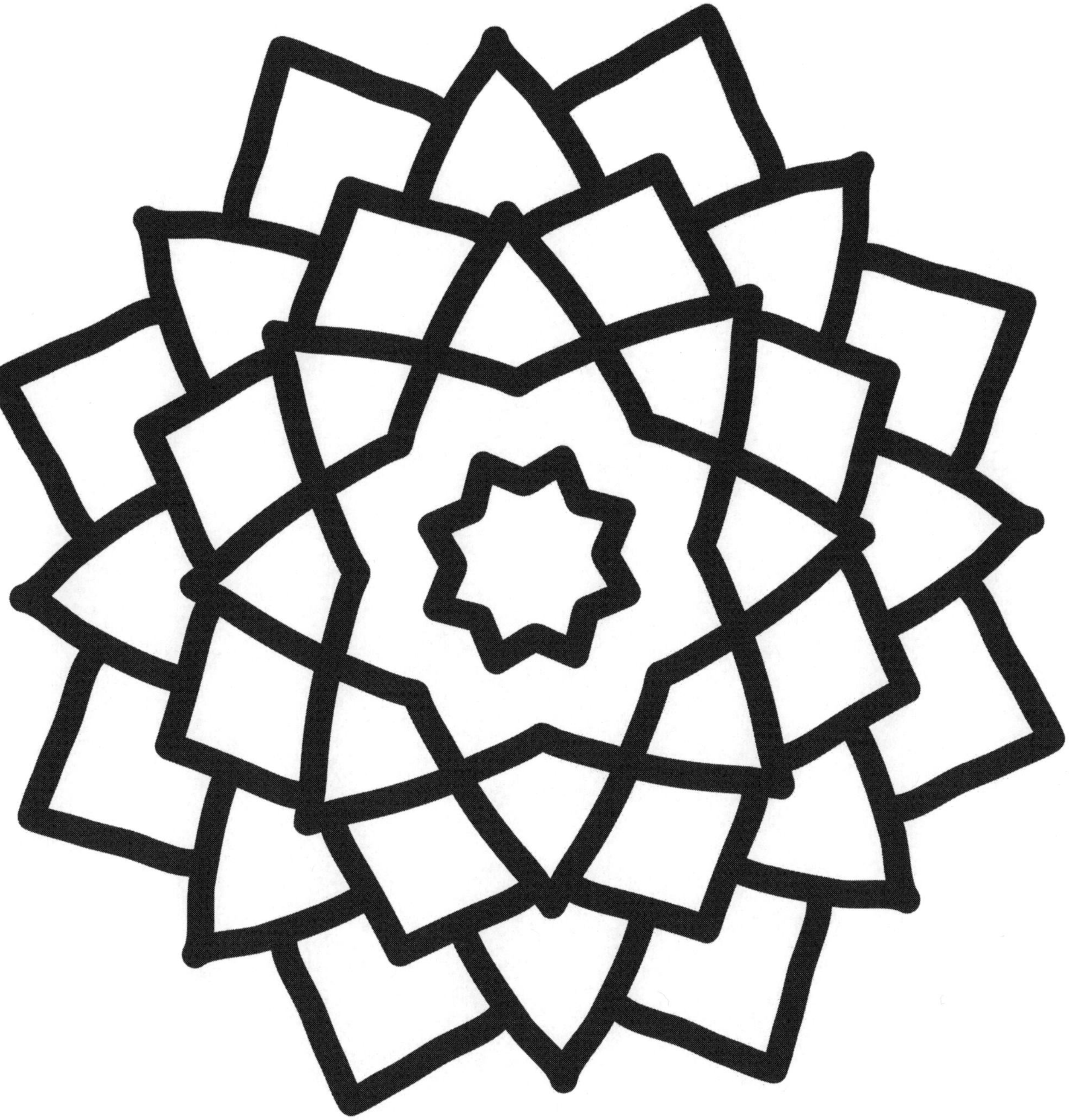

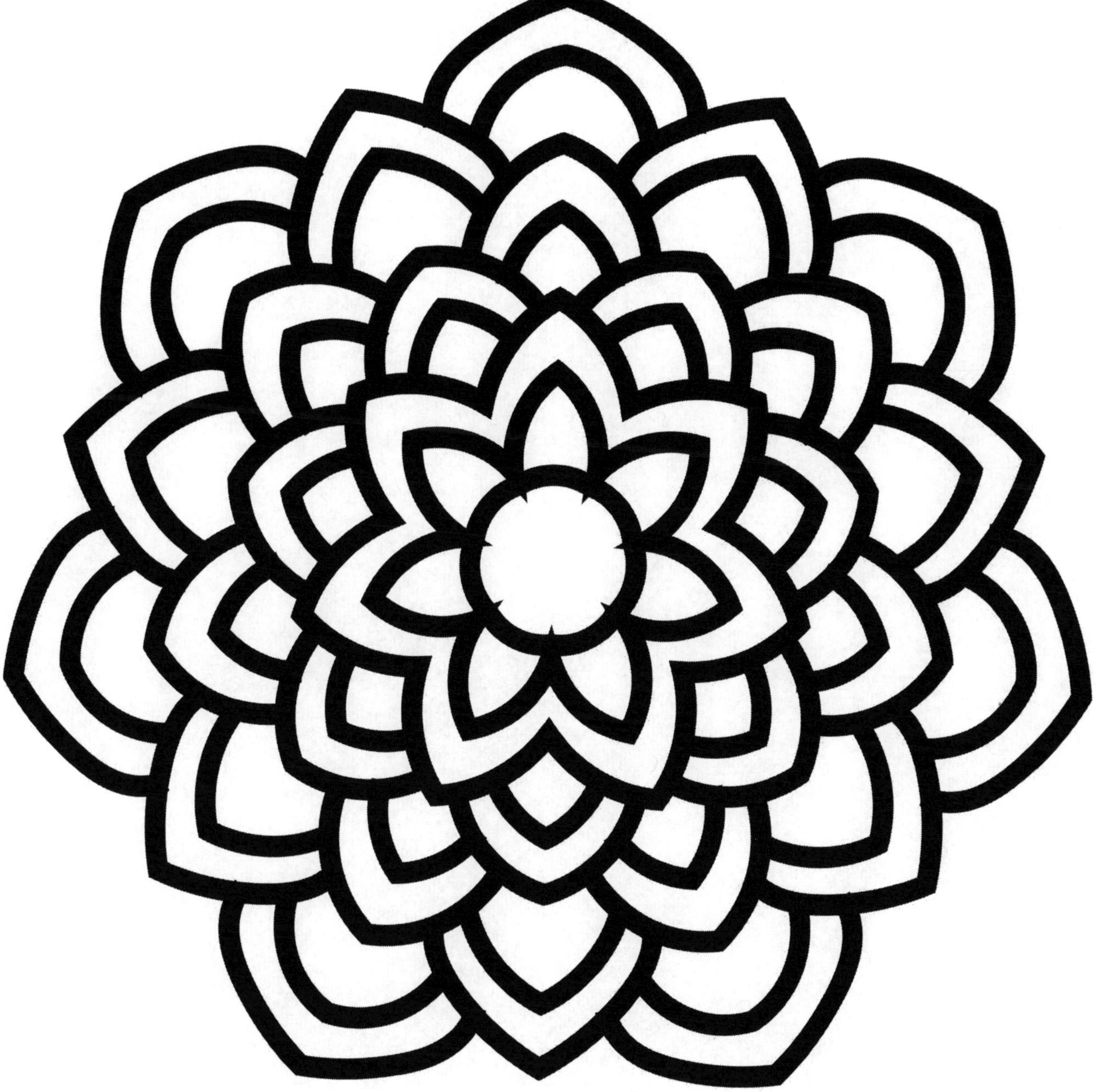

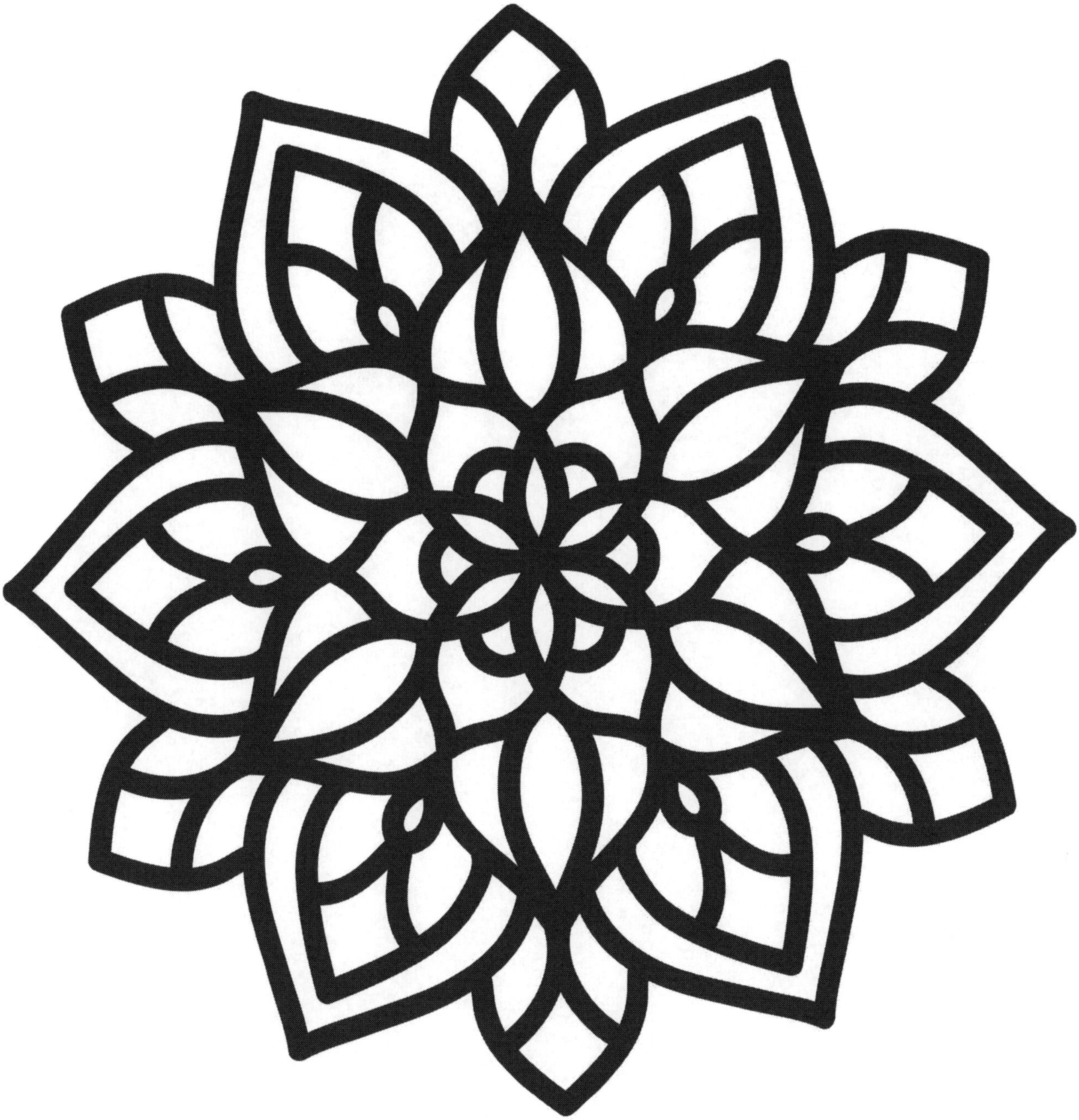

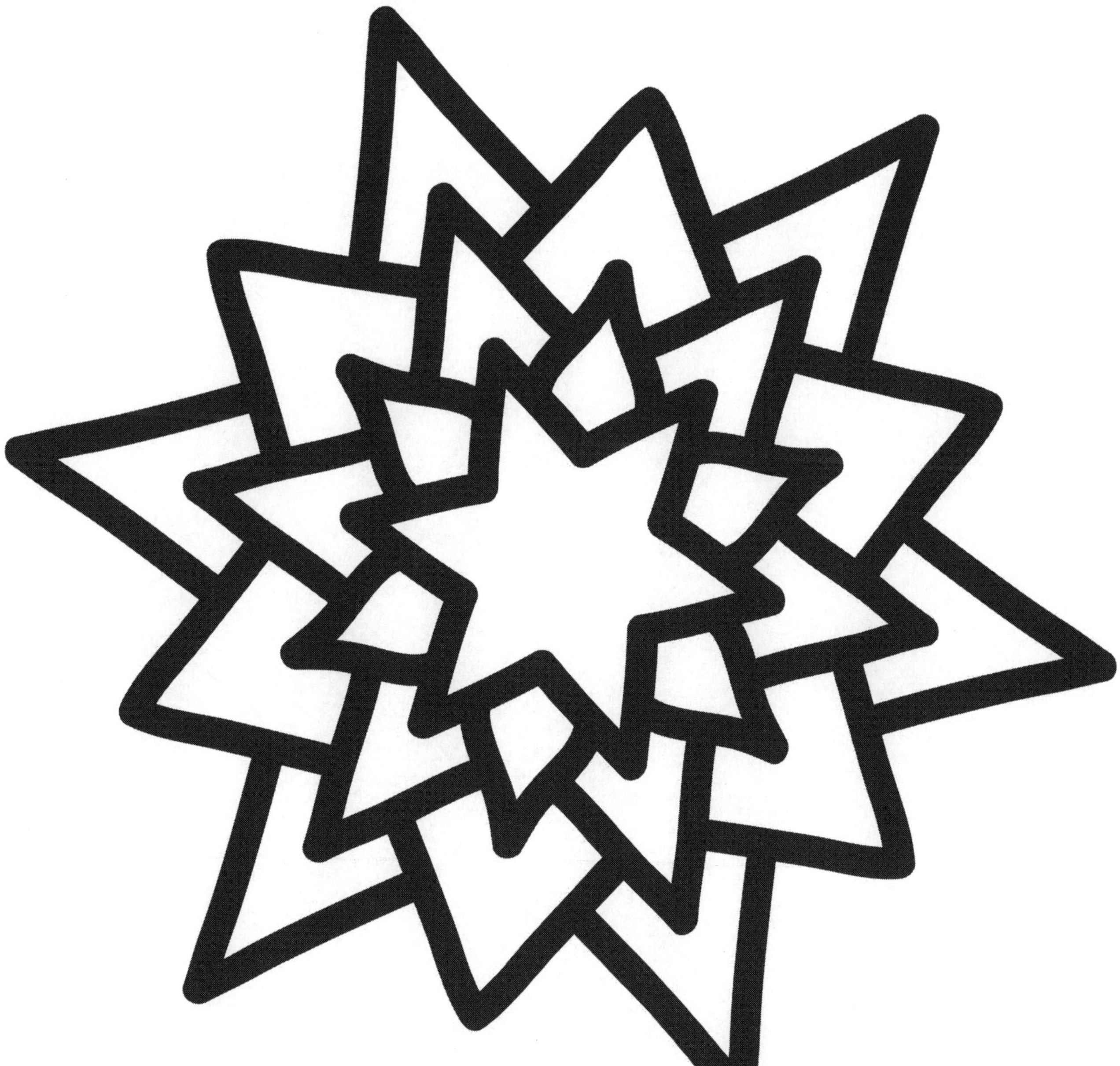

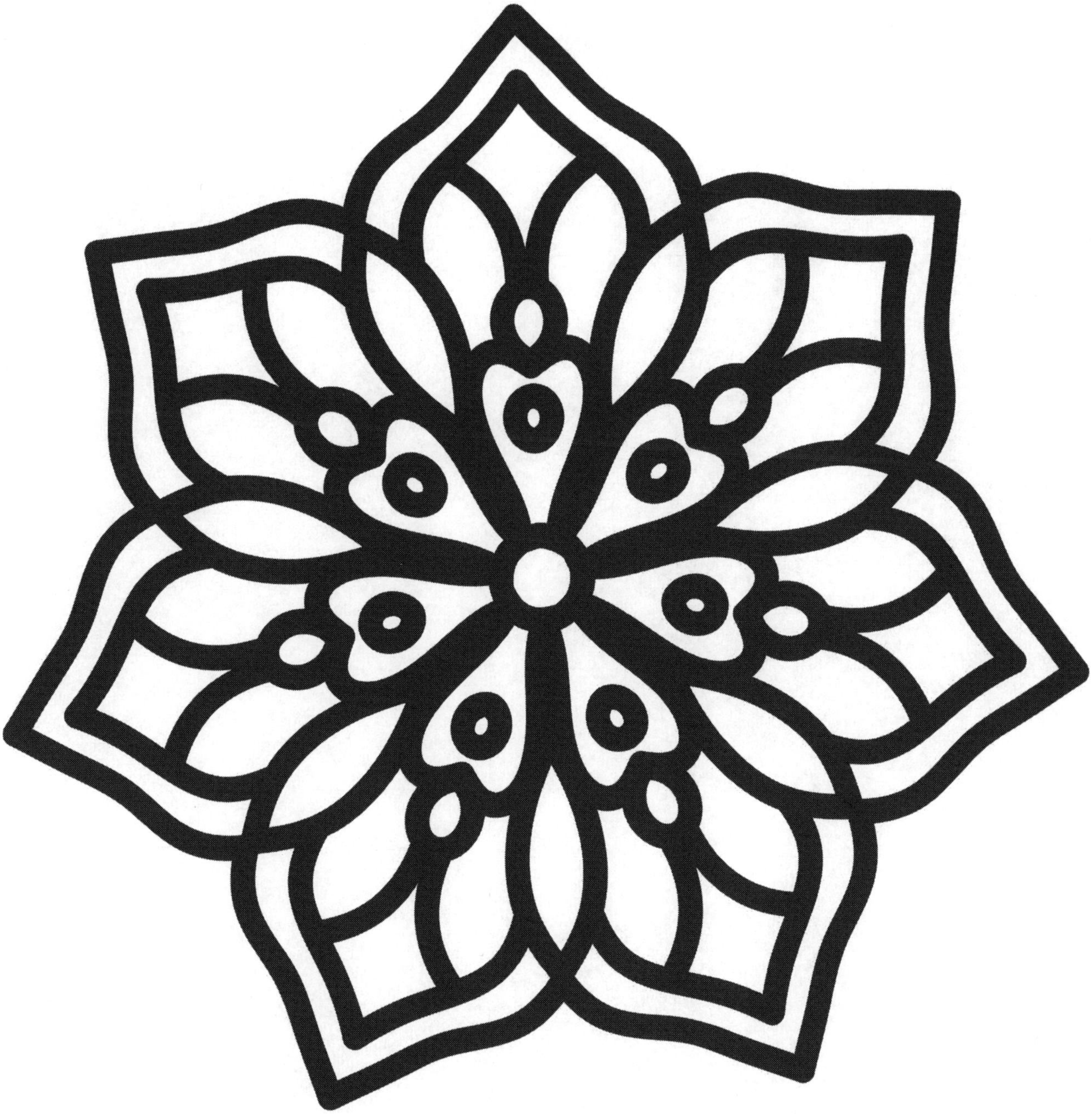

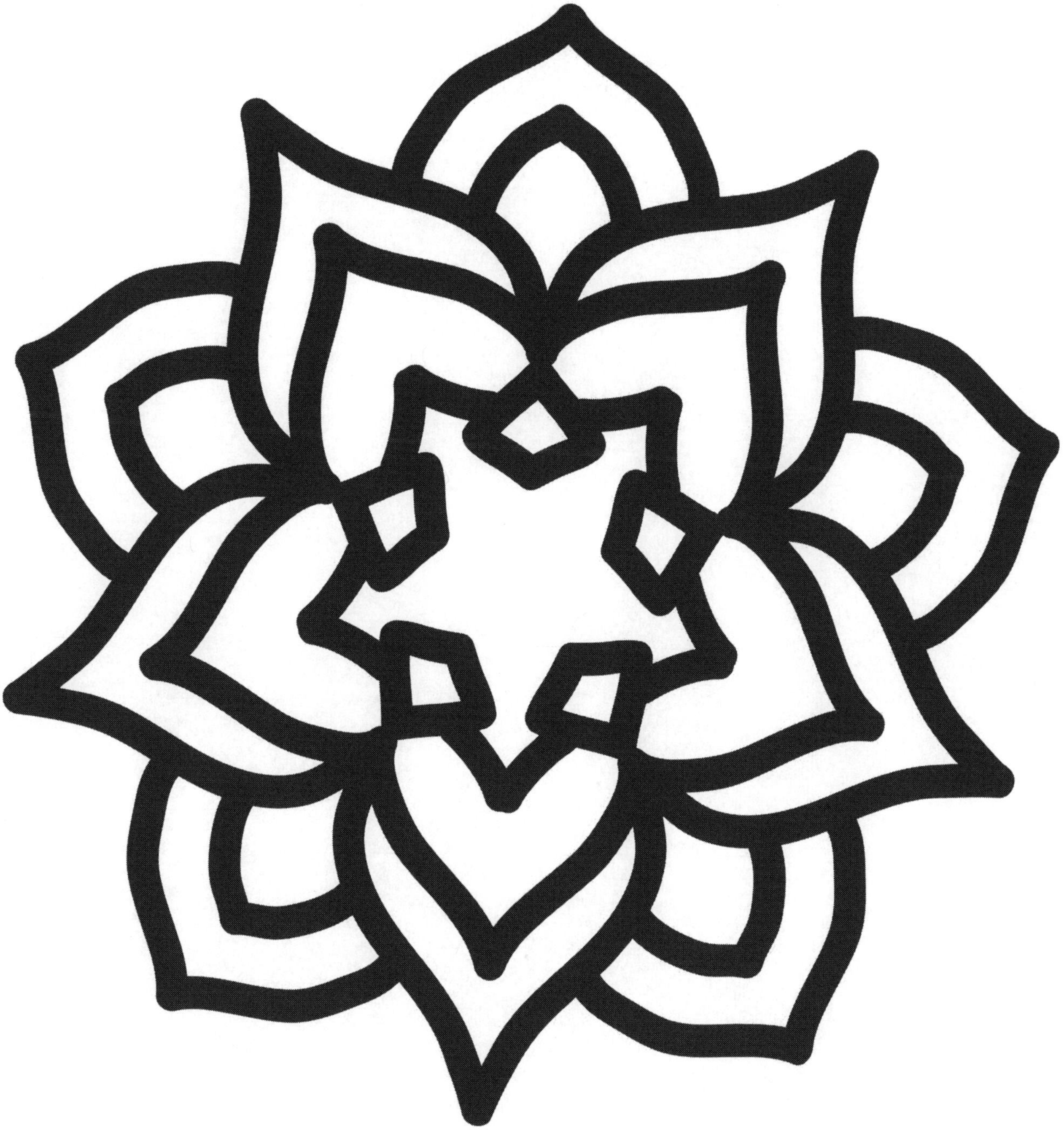

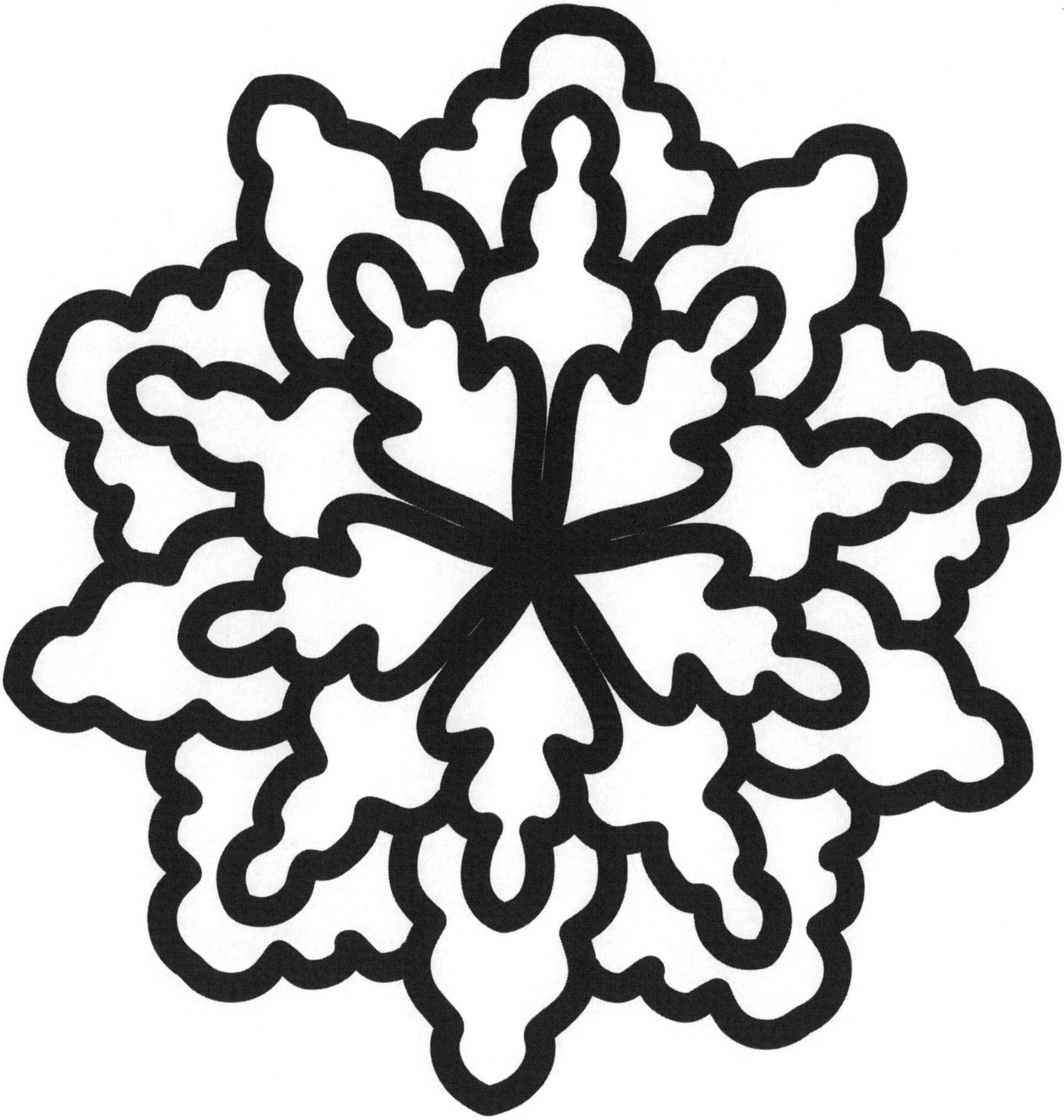

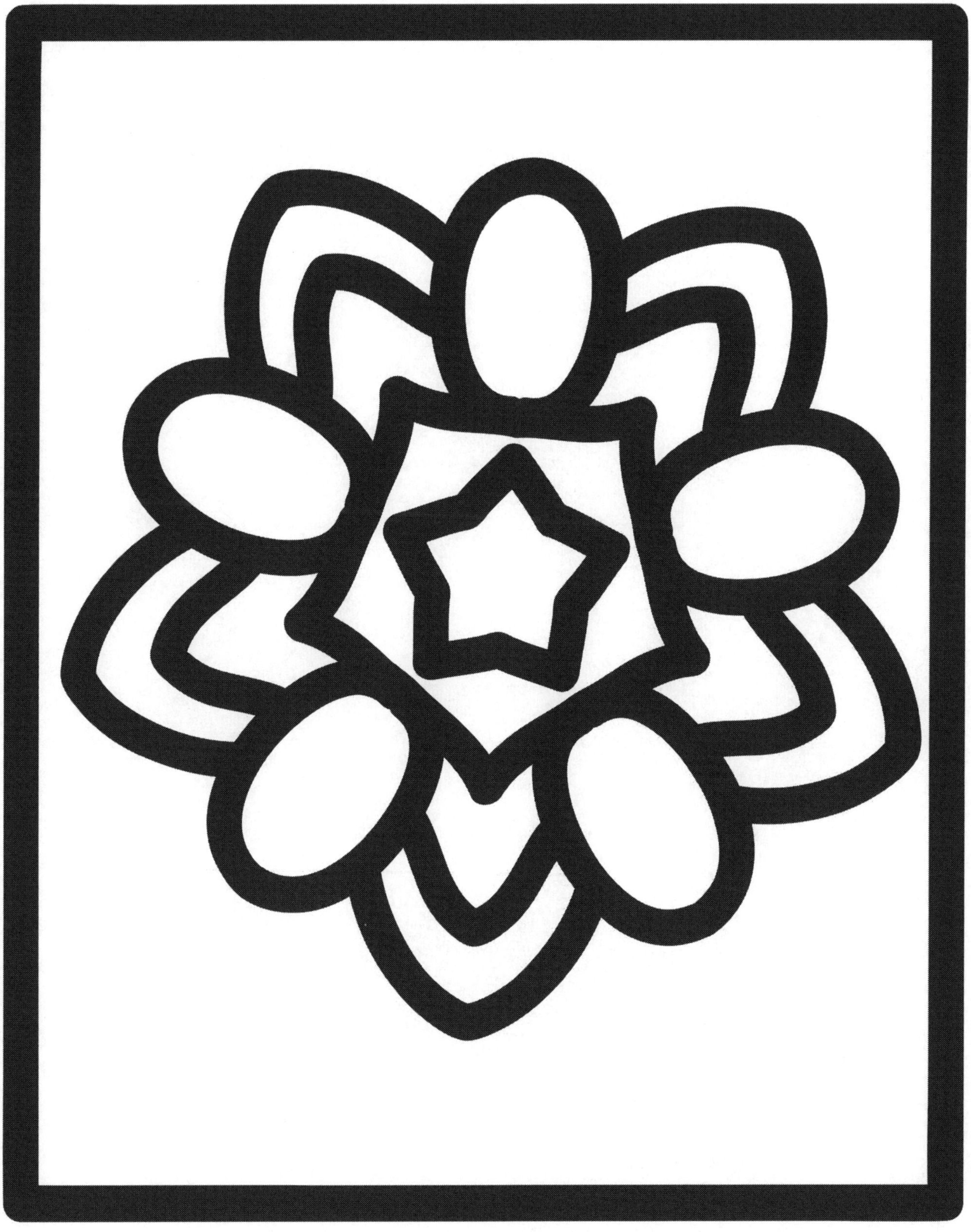

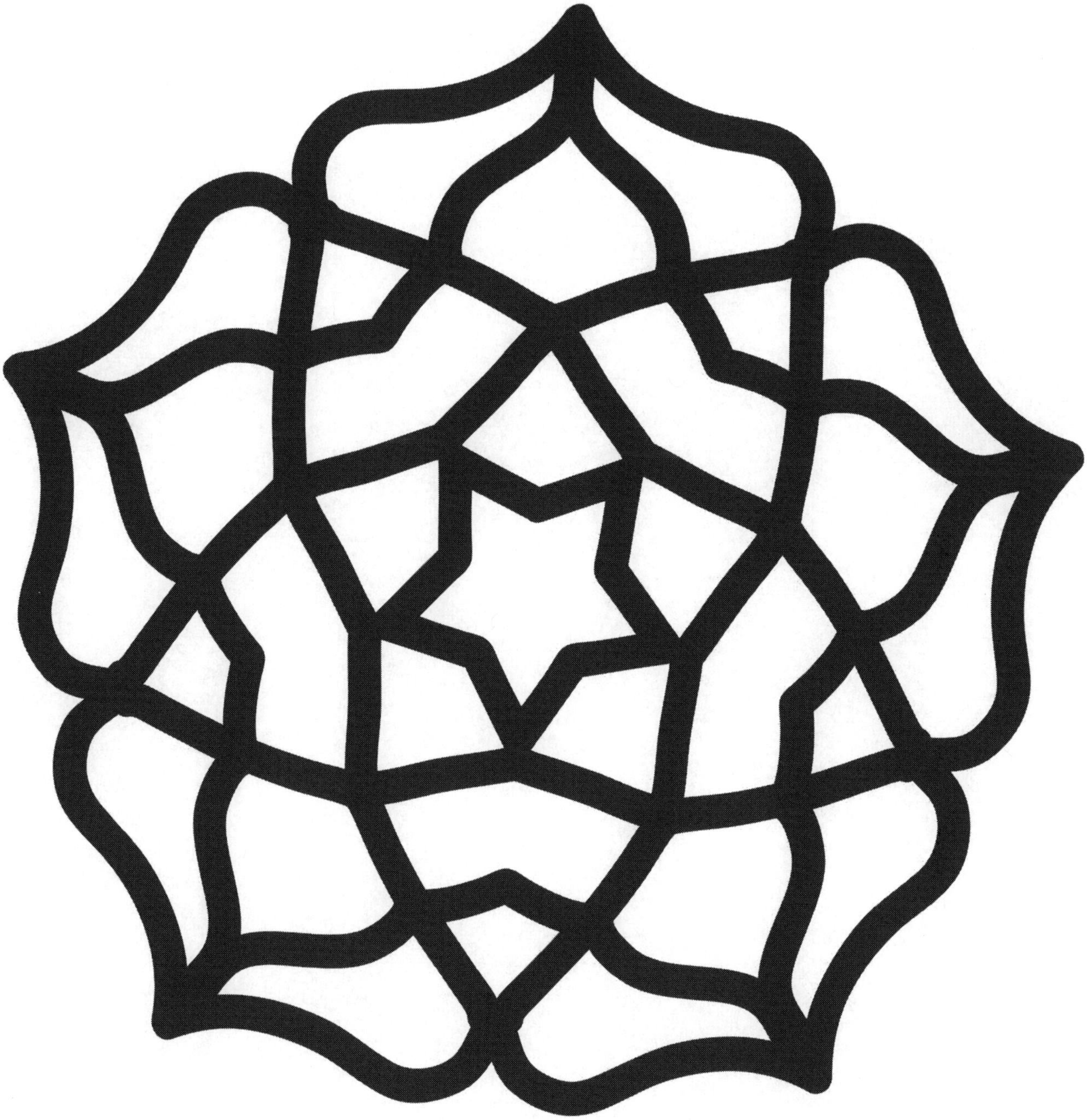

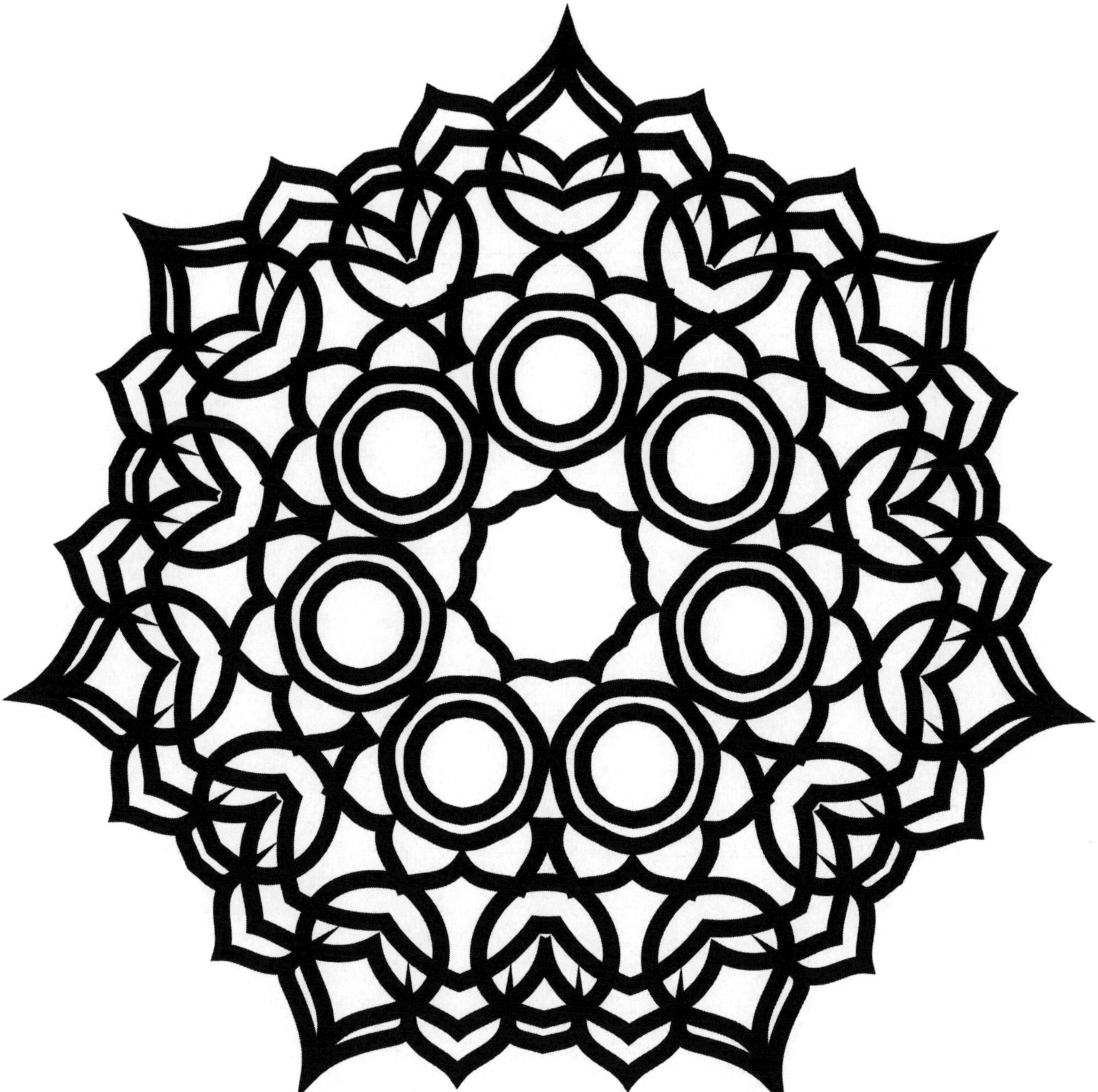

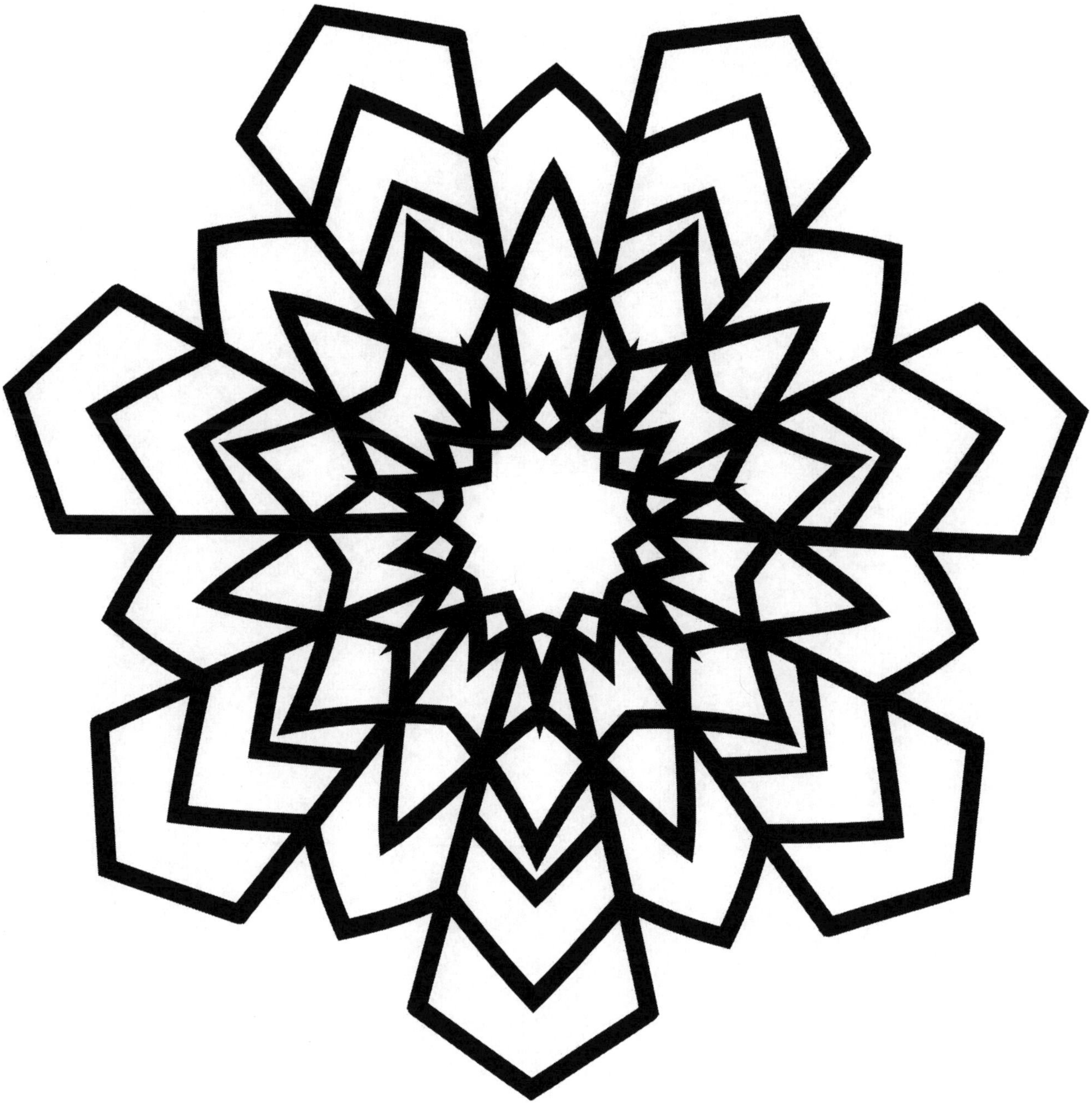

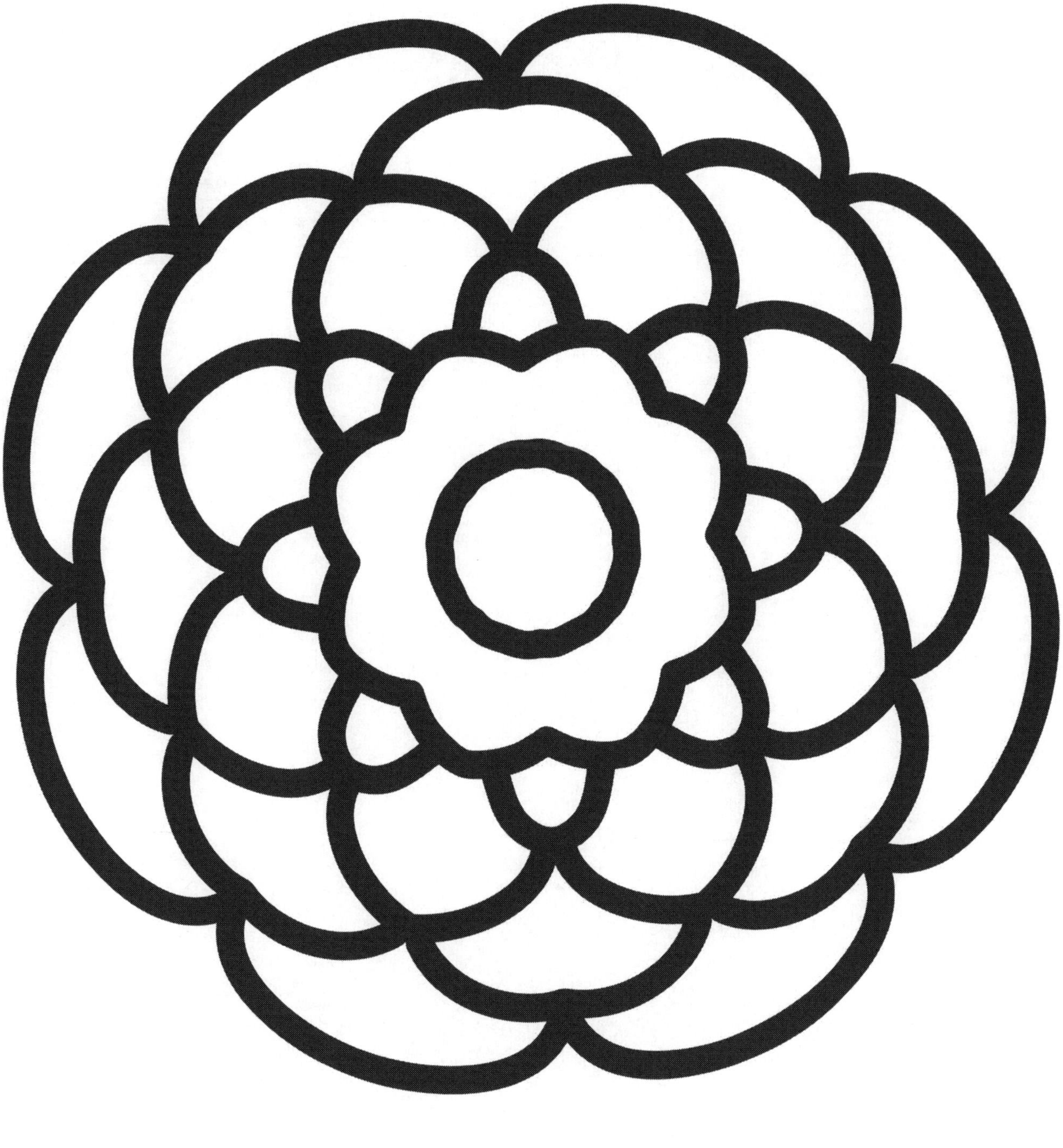

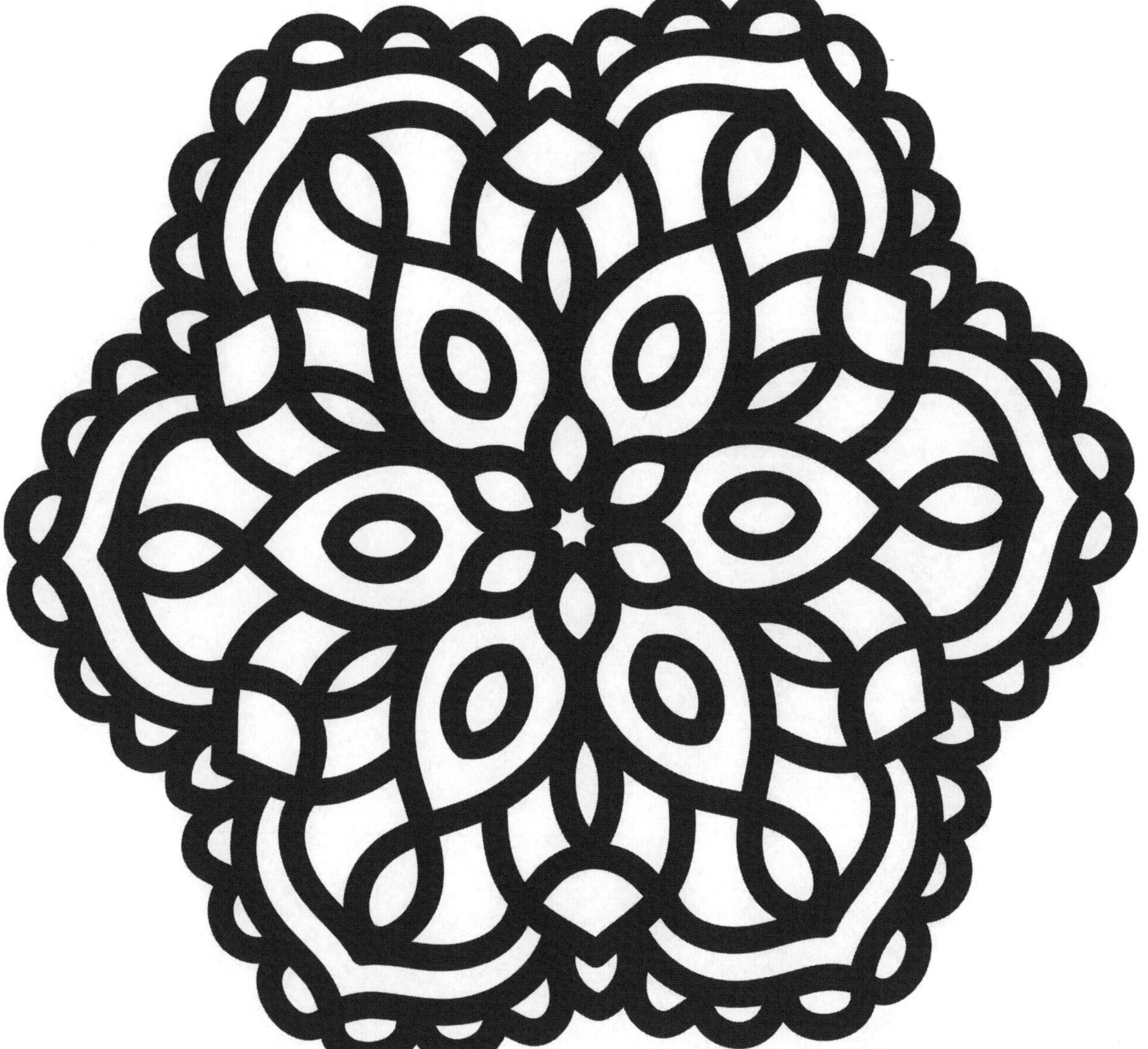

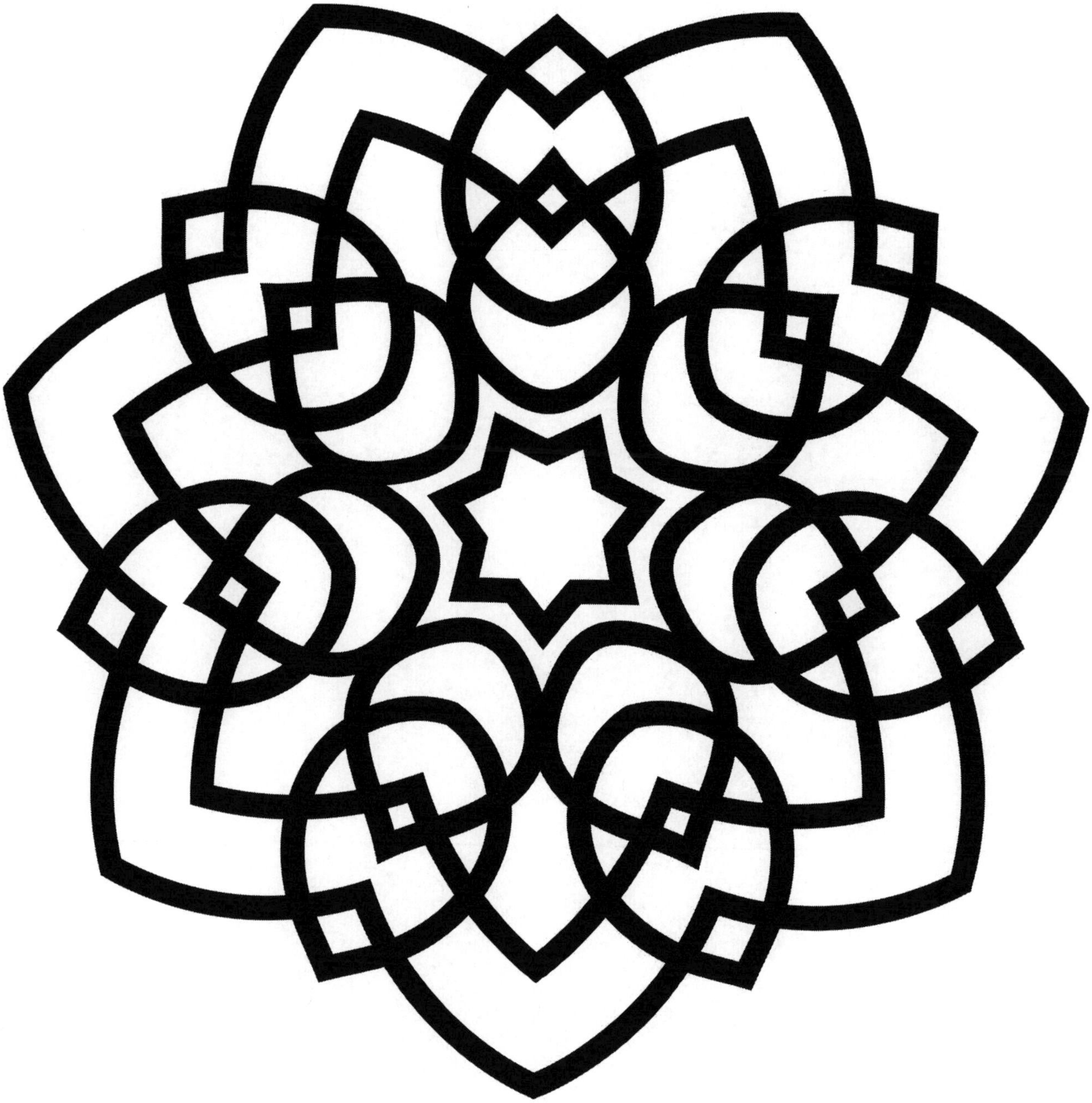

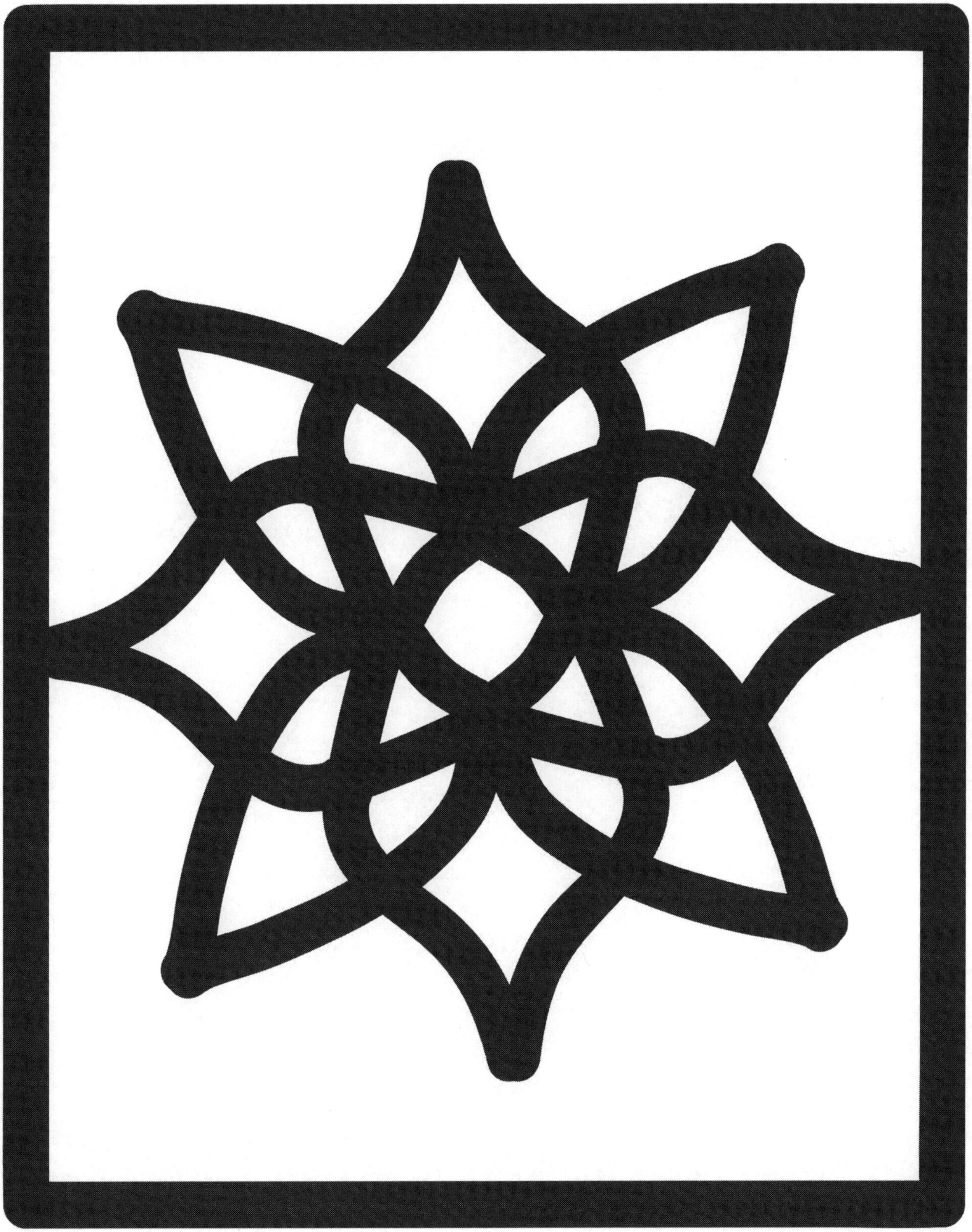

COLOR TEST PAGE

COLOR TEST PAGE

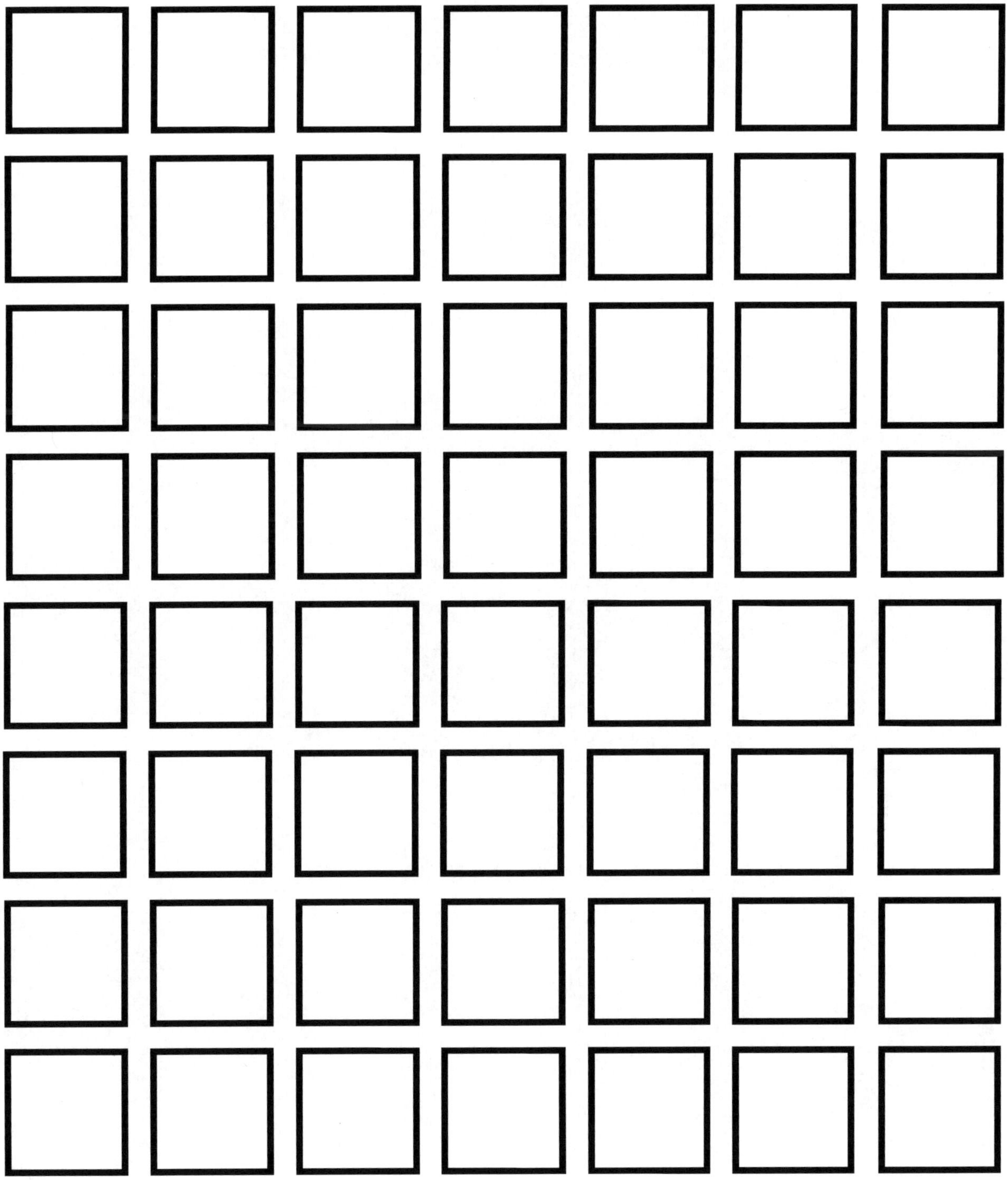

Made in the USA
Middletown, DE
11 May 2020

93949154R00038